Tasseled Jewelry

Go chic with tassels!

The jewelry designs in this easy-to-craft collection reflect a wide array of materials, from chains and leather to ribbons and beads.

LEISURE ARTS, INC. • Maumelle, Arkansas

Chain Set

Earrings

Shopping List

- ☐ Two 1" lengths of antique brass chain (ours has flat beads & cream enamel connectors)
- ☐ Embroidery floss (rose-brown, light olive & rosy peach)
- ☐ 8 8mm antique brass jump rings
- ☐ 4 4mm antique brass jump rings
- ☐ 2 antique brass ear posts
- ☐ 2 1/2" square of cardboard
- ☐ 2 pair chain-nose pliers
- ☐ E6000® industrial strength adhesive

Approx. finished length: 2 3/4" each

To make each Earring:

1. Follow *Making A Tassel* (page 31) to make 3 floss tassels (1 of each color), wrapping the cardboard about 20 times and slipping an open 8mm jump ring (page 29) through the tassel top before cutting the tassel bottom; close the jump ring.

2. Dip each tassel into warm water, being careful to not get the wrapped area and top of tassel wet. Lay flat to dry (this allows the floss strands to lie straight). Trim the tassel to 1 1/4" long.

3. Open an 8mm jump ring and slide on the 3 tassels; close the jump ring.

4. Use a 4mm jump ring to join a chain length to the jump ring on the tassels. Use a 4mm jump ring to join the remaining end of the chain length to the ear post.

TIP: *For the smoothest ends, use very sharp scissors or a rotary cutter to trim the floss.*

Necklace

Approx. finished length: 33", excluding tassels

Shopping List

- ☐ 27" length of antique brass chain (ours has flat beads & cream enamel connectors)
- ☐ 30" length of antique brass large link chain (ours has oval & square links)
- ☐ 32" length of antique brass small oval link chain (tassels go on this chain)
- ☐ Embroidery floss (rose-brown, very pale rose, light olive & rosy peach)
- ☐ 10 8mm antique brass jump rings
- ☐ 8 4mm antique brass jump rings
- ☐ antique brass lobster clasp
- ☐ 2 1/2" square of cardboard
- ☐ 2 pair chain-nose pliers
- ☐ E6000® industrial strength adhesive

To make the Necklace:

1. Follow *Making A Tassel* (page 31) to make 8 floss tassels (2 of each color), wrapping the cardboard about 20 times and slipping an open 8mm jump ring (page 29) through the tassel top before cutting the tassel bottom; close the jump ring.

2. Dip each tassel into warm water, being careful to not get the wrapped area and top of tassel wet. Lay flat to dry (this allows the floss strands to lie straight). Trim the tassel to 2 1/4" long.

3. Use an 8mm jump ring to join the three chain lengths at one end. Use an 8mm jump ring to add the lobster clasp and to join the chains at the remaining end.

4. Use a 4mm jump ring to attach each tassel to the longest chain length, centering the tassels and placing them about 1" apart.

Bracelet

Shopping List

- ☐ 6" length of antique brass chain (ours has flat beads & cream enamel connectors)
- ☐ $6^1/_2$" length of antique brass large link chain (ours has oval & square links)
- ☐ 6" length of antique brass small oval link chain
- ☐ Embroidery floss (rose-brown, light olive & rosy peach)
- ☐ 4 8mm antique brass jump rings
- ☐ 2 4mm antique brass jump rings
- ☐ antique brass toggle clasp
- ☐ $2^1/_2$" square of cardboard
- ☐ 2 pair chain-nose pliers
- ☐ E6000® industrial strength adhesive

Approx. finished length: $6^3/_4$"

TIP: *Just use longer lengths of chain to make the bracelet larger or shorter lengths to make it smaller.*

To make the Bracelet:

1. Follow *Making A Tassel* (page 31) to make 3 floss tassels (1 of each color), wrapping the cardboard about 20 times and slipping an open 8mm jump ring (page 29) through the tassel top before cutting the tassel bottom; close the jump ring.

2. Dip each tassel into warm water, being careful to not get the wrapped area and top of tassel wet. Lay flat to dry (this allows the floss strands to lie straight). Trim the tassel to $1^1/_2$" long.

3. Use a 4mm jump ring to join the three chain lengths and add the clasp ring at one end. Use a 4mm jump ring to add the clasp toggle and to join the chains at the remaining end.

4. Use an 8mm jump ring to attach the tassels to the jump ring on the clasp toggle.

Leather Earrings

Shopping List

- ☐ 6 7" lengths of dark leather cord or lace
- ☐ 6 7" lengths of light leather cord or lace
- ☐ brown iris 11/0 seed beads
- ☐ 2 14mm tigereye beads
- ☐ 2 antique bronze eye pins
- ☐ 2 7mm antique bronze jump rings
- ☐ 2 antique bronze ear wires
- ☐ monofilament illusion cord
- ☐ open loop beading needle
- ☐ round-nose pliers
- ☐ 2 pair chain-nose pliers
- ☐ wire cutters
- ☐ E6000® industrial strength adhesive
- ☐ masking tape

To make each earring:

1. Dip 3 light and 3 dark leather strips into warm water. Lay flat to dry (this removes any kinks or bends the leather may have). Thread the strips through a jump ring and bend in half.

2. To make the bead connector, slide a 14mm bead onto an eye pin. *Make a Loop* (page 29) on the wire end. Open the loops (page 29) on the bead connector to add an ear wire to one end of the connector and the leather tassel to the other end. Close the loops.

3. Securely tie one end of an 18" length of monofilament cord to one leather strip near the jump ring. Apply a drop of adhesive to the knot and let dry.

4. Slide seed beads onto the cord until the beaded area is about 6 1/2" long; place a piece of tape on the cord to keep the beads from sliding off. Tape the ear wire to the work surface. Wrap the beaded strand around the tassel top several times, concealing the jump ring. Securely tie the cord to a leather strand, hiding the knot under the beaded strand. Apply a drop of adhesive to the knot and let dry. Trim any excess cord. Glue down any beads that are not lying well.

5. Trim the leather strips as desired.

Approx. finished length: 3 3/4" each

Teardrop Necklace

Shopping List

- ☐ 20" length of silver fine link chain
- ☐ $2^3/_8$" long teardrop-shaped ring with hole at top for a head pin
- ☐ $1^3/_4$" long teardrop-shaped ring with hole at top for a head pin
- ☐ embroidery floss (very dark taupe & light taupe)
- ☐ silver head pin
- ☐ 2 6mm silver jump rings
- ☐ 3 4mm silver jump rings
- ☐ silver magnetic clasp
- ☐ round-nose pliers
- ☐ 2 pair chain-nose pliers
- ☐ wire cutters

To make the Necklace:

1. Cut 20 5" long strands of light taupe floss. Holding 4 strands together for each knot, use a Lark's Head Knot (page 31) to attach the floss to the smaller teardrop. Adjust the knots to the bottom center of the teardrop. Dip the floss into warm water. Lay flat to dry (this allows the floss strands to lie straight). Trim the strands to a point with the center about $1^1/_2$" long.

2. Cut 44 7" long strands of very dark taupe floss. Holding 4 strands together for each knot, use a Lark's Head Knot to attach the floss to the large teardrop. Adjust the knots to the bottom center of the teardrop. Dip the floss into warm water. Lay flat to dry (this allows the floss strands to lie straight). Trim the strands straight across about $2^1/_2$" long.

3. Slide the small teardrop and then the large teardrop onto the head pin. *Make a Loop* (page 29) at the top of the head pin, sliding a 4mm jump ring on before completing the loop. This completes the pendant.

4. Slide the pendant onto the chain. Attach a 4mm jump ring (page 29) to each chain end. Use the 6mm jump rings to attach the clasp to the 4mm jump rings.

Approx. finished length: $21^1/_2$", excluding pendant

TIP: *For the smoothest ends, use very sharp scissors or a rotary cutter to trim the floss ends.*

Ladder Necklace

Shopping List

- ☐ 4 packages of 72" lengths of gold small link chain (or a total of 270" of chain)
- ☐ 54 7mm x 7mm turquoise square 2-hole glass beads
- ☐ 48 6mm turquoise faceted glass beads
- ☐ gold magnetic clasp
- ☐ 28 gold eye pins
- ☐ 2 4mm gold jump rings
- ☐ round-nose pliers
- ☐ 2 pair chain-nose pliers
- ☐ wire cutters

To make the Necklace:

1. Thread 6 faceted beads on an eye pin. *Make a Loop* (page 29) at the wire end. Repeat to make a total of 8 beaded eye pins.

2. Thread 6 square beads on 2 eye pins. Make a loop at each wire end. Repeat to make a total of 9 beaded eye pins.

3. Cut two 22" chain lengths. Use the jump rings (page 29) to attach a clasp piece to one end of each chain length.

4. Lay the chain on a flat work surface and align the links so they are parallel to each other. Attach a square-bead beaded eye pin about 5" from each end of the chain lengths. Be sure you are attaching the eye pins to the same link on each side of the chain; this ensures the beads hang straight. Attach a round-bead beaded eye pin to the chain right above the square-bead eye pin. Continue to add beaded eye pins, alternating bead type until you have used all the beaded eye pins.

5. Cut 48 4 1/2" chain lengths. Thread each chain length on 2 eye pins. Attach the eye pins to the necklace just below the bottom beaded eye pin.

Approx. finished length: 24", excluding beads & fringe

Dip Dye Set

Earrings

Approx. finished length: 4" each

Shopping List

- ☐ 2 2" lengths of gold small link chain
- ☐ 2 gold metal findings with multiple holes/ loops
- ☐ 6 4mm gold jump rings
- ☐ 2 gold ear wires
- ☐ 1 skein white embroidery floss
- ☐ desired color liquid dye
- ☐ small bowl about 3" deep
- ☐ 2 pair chain-nose pliers
- ☐ disposable gloves & paper towels

To make each earring:

1. For each "fringe," cut 3 7" lengths of floss. Use a Lark's Head Knot (page 31) to attach each floss grouping to a metal finding.

2. Refer to *Dip Dye Necklace*, page 15, Step 2, to dye the fringe.

3. Once the fringe is completely dry, use jump rings (page 29) to join a chain length to a metal finding.

4. Use a jump ring to attach an ear wire to the center of the chain length.

Necklace

Shopping List

- ☐ 28"l gold small link chain
- ☐ 6 5mm x 3mm pink rondelle beads
- ☐ 3 gold metal findings with multiple holes/loops
- ☐ 4mm gold jump rings to join metal findings (we used 6)
- ☐ 6 gold eye pins
- ☐ 2 skeins white embroidery floss
- ☐ desired color liquid dye
- ☐ small bowl about 3" deep
- ☐ round-nose pliers
- ☐ 2 pair chain-nose pliers
- ☐ wire cutters
- ☐ disposable gloves & paper towels

To make the Necklace:

1. For each "fringe," cut 3 8" lengths of floss. Use a Lark's Head Knot (page 31) to attach each floss grouping to the metal findings.

2. Keeping the knotted areas dry, dip the fringe into clear water. Follow the manufacturer's instructions to dilute the dye. Fill the bowl with 1" of dye. Dip the fringe into the dye solution, stopping about 1/4" below the knotted area. The dye will move up the wet floss, stopping where the floss is dry. Referring to **Fig. 1**, let the fringe soak in the dye for a few minutes. Lay flat on a paper towel to dry.

3. Once fringe is completely dry, use jump rings to join the metal findings, completing the pendant. Trim the fringe as desired.

4. To make a bead connector, slide a pink bead onto an eye pin. *Make a Loop* (page 29) at the wire end. Make 6 bead connectors. Open the loops (page 29) on the connectors to join 3 bead connectors to either side of the pendant; close the loops. Join the chain to the bead connectors.

Fig. 1

Approx. finished length: 30", excluding pendant

Bag Tassels

Beaded

Shopping List

- ☐ 3 colors flat suede lace cord (9 feet of each)
- ☐ 4 24mm assorted color ceramic beads
- ☐ 13 16mm assorted color ceramic beads
- ☐ 9 10mm silver beads
- ☐ 2 6mm assorted color beads
- ☐ 3 9" lengths of silver chunky chain
- ☐ 6 24mm silver split rings
- ☐ 32mm silver split ring
- ☐ silver crimp beads
- ☐ stringing wire
- ☐ crimping tool
- ☐ wire cutters
- ☐ E6000® industrial strength adhesive

Approx. finished length: 9"-10" each

To make the Tassel:

1. Cut 6 16" lengths and a 6" length of each suede cord color. Dip suede lengths into water. Lay flat to dry (this removes any kinks or bends the suede may have).

2. For a suede tassel, thread the 16" suede lengths (all of one color) through a 24mm split ring and bend in half. Wrap the suede just below the ring with the matching 6" length; tuck the ends into the wraps, glue in place, and trim the excess.

3. Repeat Step 2 to make a total of 3 suede tassels.

4. Cut a 24" length of stringing wire. Alternating sizes, thread 5 16mm beads and 4 24mm beads on the wire. Thread a 6mm bead on the wire. Skipping the 6mm bead, thread the wire back through the beads. Thread on a crimp bead and a 24mm split ring and thread. Thread the wire back through the crimp bead and several of the beads. Secure the crimp bead (page 30). Trim the excess wire.

5. Repeat Step 5 to make another beaded tassel, alternating silver beads and the remaining 16mm beads.

6. Attach each chain length to the last 24mm split ring. Attach all 24mm split rings to the 32mm split ring. Attach to your bag.

Fabric

Shopping List

- ☐ 10" x 17" piece of tightly woven cotton fabric (we used a blue, grey, green & brown batik print)
- ☐ $1^7/_8$ yards of $^3/_{16}$" wide aqua braided trim
- ☐ $1^5/_8$ yards of $^3/_{16}$" wide studded suede trim
- ☐ 24mm silver split ring
- ☐ very large silver lobster clasp
- ☐ E6000® industrial strength adhesive

To make the Tassel:

1. Cut 18 $^1/_2$" x 16" strips of fabric. Cut 4 16" lengths of braided trim. Cut 3 16" lengths of suede trim. Cut a 6" length of suede trim.

2. Thread all the fabric strips through the split ring and bend in half. Repeat with the aqua and suede trim lengths. Wrap the tassel just below the ring with the 6" suede trim length; tuck the ends into the wraps, glue in place, and trim the excess.

3. Attach the clasp to the split ring. Trim the ends as desired.

Gold Earrings

Shopping List

- ☐ 2 2"l gold tassels (we cut ours from a length of trim from the home dec section, leaving a small loop to attach the jump rings)
- ☐ 2 19mm beads with attached bead caps
- ☐ 50-56 gold 11/0 seed beads
- ☐ 2 2" lengths of gold 3/8"w ribbon
- ☐ monofilament illusion cord
- ☐ 2 4mm gold jump rings
- ☐ 2 gold eye pins
- ☐ 2 gold ear wires
- ☐ open-loop beading needle
- ☐ round-nose pliers
- ☐ 2 pair chain-nose pliers
- ☐ wire cutters
- ☐ E6000® industrial strength adhesive

To make each Earring:

1. Cut a 12" length of monofilament cord. Thread through the beading needle and knot one end. Thread the needle from back to front through one ribbon length close to one end. Adhere the ribbon and cord to the top of one tassel ***(Fig. 1)***.

2. Wrap the ribbon around the tassel top, trim any excess, and adhere in place. Slide enough seed beads on the monofilament cord to wrap around the tassel top. Wrap the seed beads around the tassel top and tightly knot the cord. Place a drop of adhesive on the knot to secure. Slide the threaded needle through the tassel. Trim the excess cord.

3. To make the bead connector, slide a 19mm bead onto an eye pin. *Make a Loop* (page 29) at the wire end.

4. Open a 4mm jump ring (page 29) and slide on the tassel as well as the bead connector; close the jump ring.

5. Attach the ear wire to the remaining loop on the bead connector.

Fig. 1

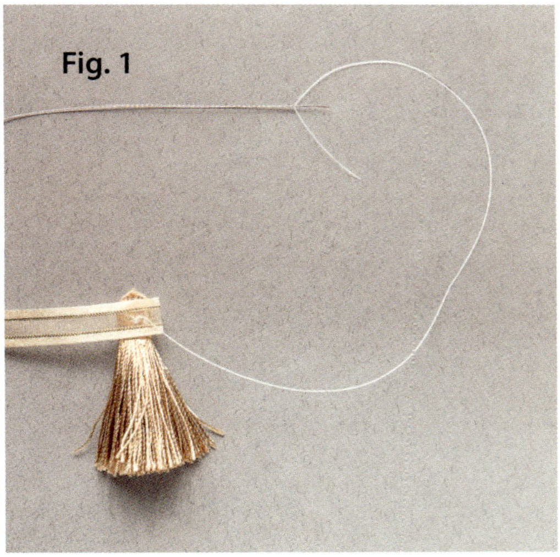

Approx. finished length: 2 7/8" each

Spiky Earrings

Shopping List

- ☐ Two 1" lengths of antique brass small link chain
- ☐ Two 1 1/4" lengths of antique brass small link chain
- ☐ 18 assorted metal top-loop spikes
- ☐ 18 4mm antique brass jump rings
- ☐ 2 8mm antique brass jump rings
- ☐ 2 antique brass ear wires
- ☐ 2 pair chain-nose pliers

To make each Earring:

1. Use 4mm jump rings (page 29) to attach 5 spikes to a 1 1/4" chain length and 4 spikes to a 1" chain length, spacing the spikes evenly along each chain length.

2. Open an 8mm jump ring and slide on the spiked chain lengths and an ear wire. Close the jump ring.

Approx. finished length: 2 1/2" each

TIP: *We were lucky enough to find the metal spikes already on a chain length, making these lightening fast to put together!*

Stone Pendant Necklace

Shopping List

- ☐ 2 12" lengths of black small link chain
- ☐ 15mm amber faceted glass bead
- ☐ 40mm natural stone bead (we used an agate slice bead)
- ☐ 23"-25" length of 4mm x 4mm x 1mm square hematite rondelle beads
- ☐ 5 bronze 11/0 seed beads
- ☐ 5 4mm antique bronze jump rings
- ☐ 4 5mm black jump rings
- ☐ black spring ring clasp
- ☐ black eye pin
- ☐ monofilament illusion cord
- ☐ open loop beading needle
- ☐ round-nose pliers
- ☐ 2 pair chain-nose pliers
- ☐ wire cutters
- ☐ E6000® industrial strength adhesive

To make the Necklace:

1. To make a bead strand for the tassel, thread about 4 1/2"-5" of square rondelle beads onto a 15" length of monofilament cord. Thread on a bronze seed bead and thread the needle back through all the square beads. Securely knot the cord to a 4mm jump ring and apply a drop of adhesive to the knot. When dry, trim the excess cord. Repeat this process to make a total of 5 bead strands.

2. Slide the bead strands to the center of an 8" length of monofilament cord. Feed the cord ends through the stone bead. Securely tie a 5mm jump ring to the pendant right above the stone bead. Apply a drop of adhesive to the knot. When dry, trim the excess cord.

3. To make the bead connector, slide the 15mm bead onto the eye pin and *Make a Loop* (page 29).

4. Use the 5mm jump rings to join a clasp piece to one end on each chain length. Use a 5mm jump ring to join the remaining chain ends to one end of the bead connector.

5. Join the pendant to the bead connector.

Approx. finished length: 25", excluding pendant

Wrap Necklace

Approx. finished length: 80 1/2"

Shopping List

- ☐ 16 10mm glass beads
- ☐ 68 6mm glass beads
- ☐ 194 4mm AB (aurora borialis) finish faceted glass beads
- ☐ amber 6/0 seed beads
- ☐ light brown waxed cord (be sure it will fit through 10mm, 6mm & 4mm bead holes)
- ☐ 2 6mm gold jump rings
- ☐ 2 gold jewelry cones
- ☐ 2 gold metal cord ends with loop
- ☐ monofilament illusion cord
- ☐ open loop beading needle
- ☐ 2 pair chain-nose pliers
- ☐ E6000® industrial strength adhesive

To make the Necklace:

1. Cut a 150" length of waxed cord. Tie an overhand knot (page 30) at the cord center.

2. Tying an overhand knot between each bead and keeping the knots close to the beads (page 30), thread on 55 4mm beads; tie an overhand knot close to the last bead.

3. Tying an overhand knot between each bead, keeping the knots close to the beads, and alternating the 6mm and 4mm beads, thread on 34 6mm beads and 33 4mm beads. You'll end with a 6mm bead. Tie an overhand knot close to the last bead.

4. Alternating the 4mm and 10mm beads, thread on 9 4mm beads and 8 10mm beads.

5. Trim the waxed cord end to just a bit over 1/4". Place a drop of adhesive in a metal cord end. Insert the waxed cord end all the way into the metal cord end and allow to dry.

6. Repeat Steps 2-5 for the opposite side of the necklace.

7. To make the bead strands for a tassel, thread about 6" of gold seed beads onto a 20" length of monofilament cord. Skipping the bead closest the needle, thread the needle back through all the other beads. Being sure to leave a bit of slack in the cord and skipping the bead closest to the needle, thread the needle back through 5-6 beads. Knot the cord with several small knots and apply a drop of adhesive to the knots. Trim the excess cord. Repeat this process to make a total of 8 bead strands.

8. Lay the 8 bead strands side by side. Slide a 14" length of monofilament cord under the center of the bead strands ***(Fig. 1)*** and tie a secure knot. Add a drop of adhesive to the knot and allow to dry.

9. Feed the cord ends through a jewelry cone and then through a jump ring. Tie a secure knot. Add a drop of adhesive to the knot and allow to dry. Trim the excess cord and tuck the knot in to the cone.

10. Open the jump ring (page 29) and slide one metal cord end onto the jump ring. Close the jump ring.

11. Repeat Steps 7-10 to make and add the remaining beaded tassel to the opposite end of the necklace.

Fig. 1

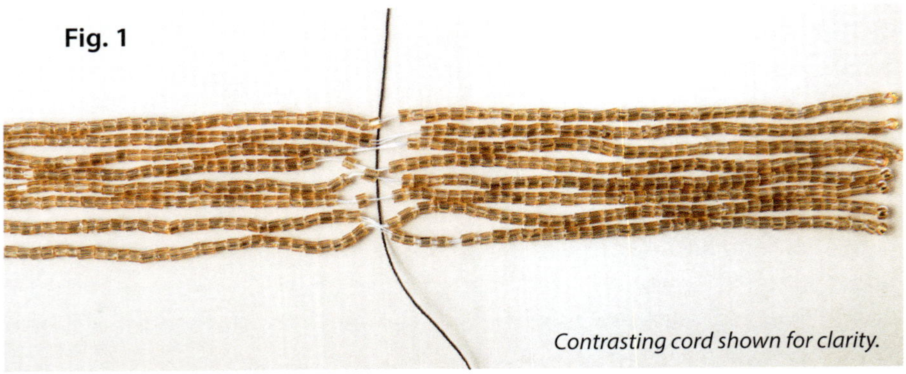

Contrasting cord shown for clarity.

General Instructions

TOOLS

Chain-nose pliers have rounded, tapered jaws and a flat interior surface that will not mar wire. These pliers are used for reaching into tight places, gripping objects, opening and closing jump rings, and bending wire.

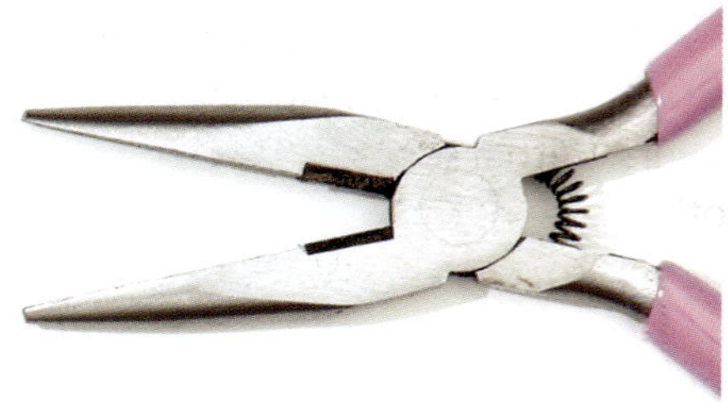

Round-nose pliers have round jaws that are useful for making loops and bending wire smoothly.

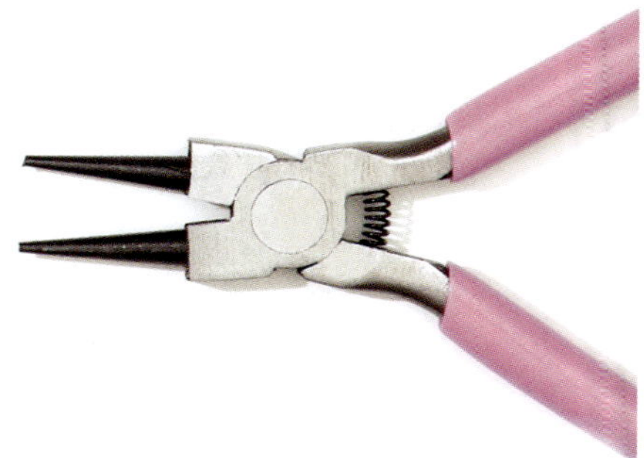

Wire cutters are used to cut small gauge wire, head pins, and eye pins.

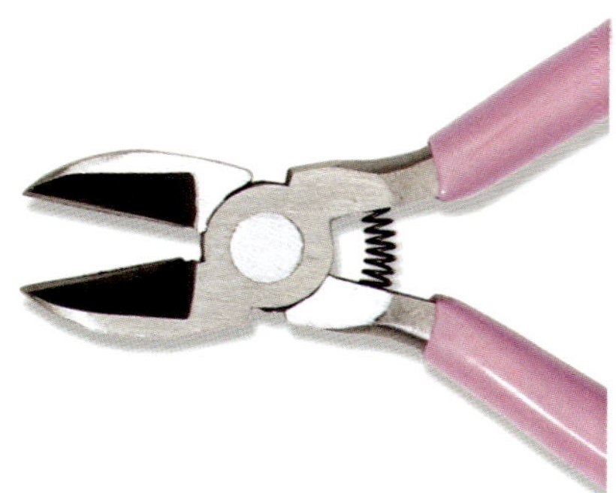

A crimp tool (also known as crimping pliers) flattens and shapes the crimp bead or crimp tube.

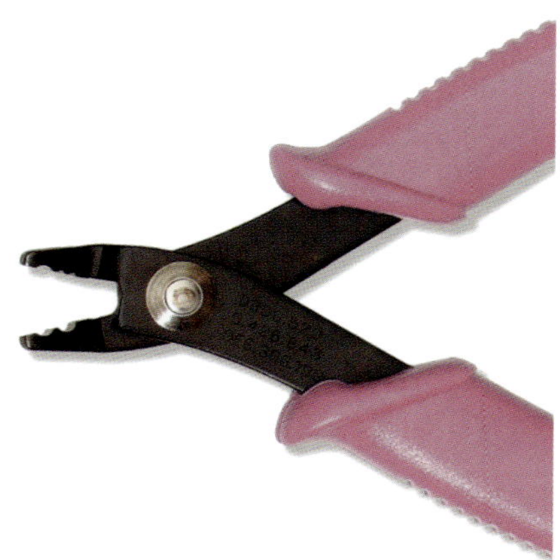

TECHNIQUES

Opening and Closing Jump Rings, Loops, or Chain Links

Hold one side of the jump ring, loop, or link with chain-nose pliers. With a second pair of chain-nose pliers, gently hold the other side of the jump ring. Open the ring by pulling one pair of pliers toward you while pushing the other away *(Fig. 1)*.

Fig. 1

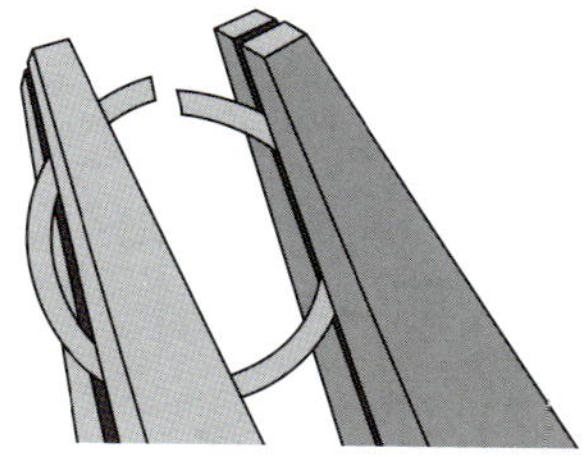

Close the ring by pushing and pulling the pliers in opposite directions, bringing the ring ends back together.

Making a Loop on a Head Pin or Eye Pin

Slide the bead(s) on a head pin or eye pin. Leaving about 1/2", cut off the excess wire. Using chain-nose pliers, bend the wire at a 90° angle *(Fig. 2)*. Grasp the wire end with the round-nose pliers. Turn the pliers and bend the wire into a loop *(Figs. 3-4)*. Release the pliers. Straighten or twist the loop further if necessary.

Fig. 2

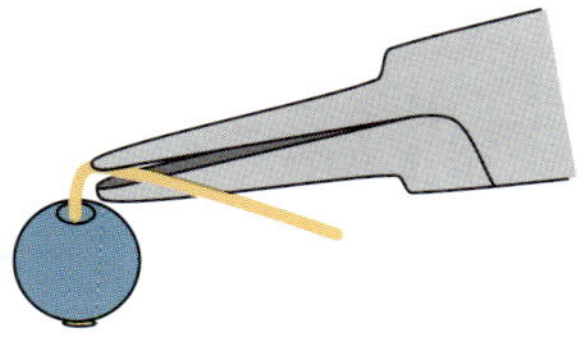

Fig. 3

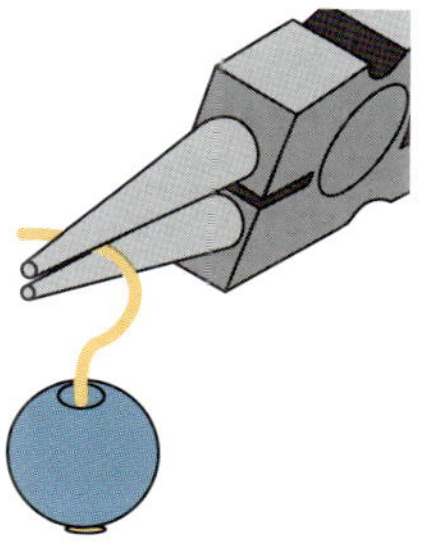

Fig. 4

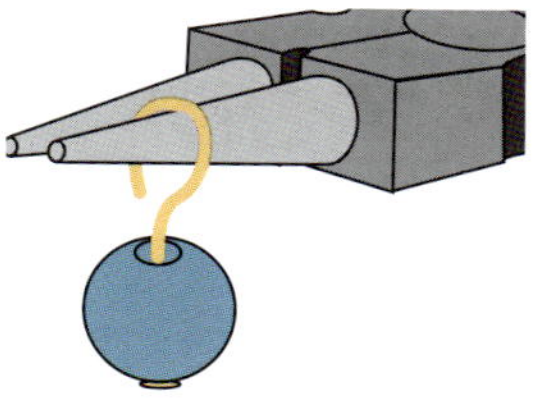

Using Crimp Beads
To finish a wire end, thread a crimp bead and the clasp or jump ring on the wire. Run the wire back through the crimp bead; use a pair of chain-nose pliers to pull and tighten the wire ***(Fig. 5)***. Place the crimp bead on the inner groove of the crimp tool and squeeze ***(Fig. 6)***.

Fig. 5

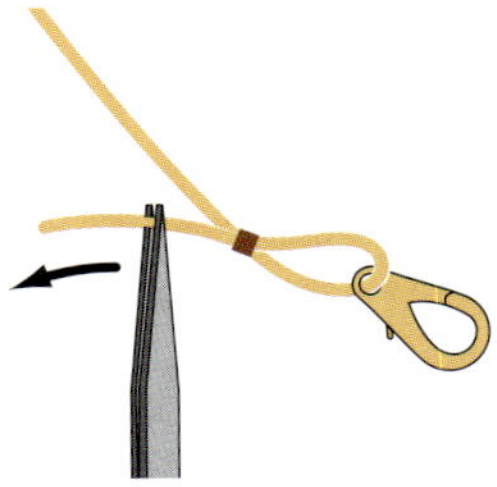

Fig. 6

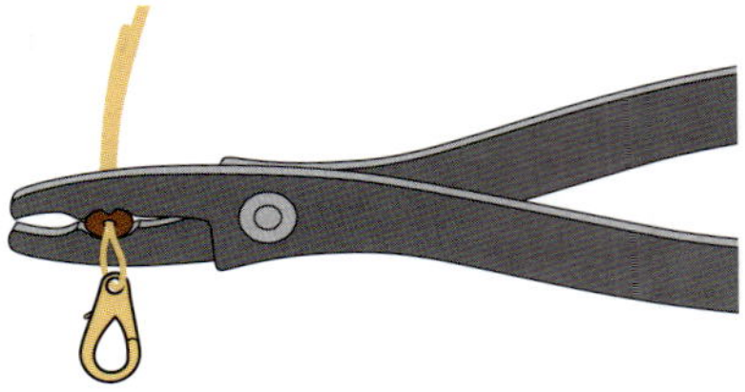

Release the tool, turn the crimp bead a quarter turn, and place it in the outer groove ***(Fig. 7)***. Squeeze the tool to round out the crimp bead ***(Fig. 8)***. Trim the wire end or if the design calls for beads, thread the beads over the wire to cover the end.

Fig. 7

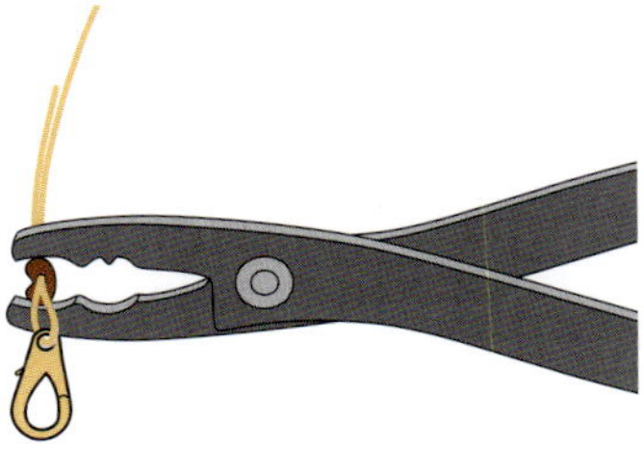

Fig. 8

Tying An Overhand Knot
This simple knot often begins and ends a beaded strand and can be used to join components ***(Fig. 9)***.

Fig. 9

Tying Knots Between Beads
As you tie an overhand knot, slip a straight pin in the knot loop and guide the knot as close to the bead as possible ***(Fig. 10)***.

Fig. 10

Lark's Head Knot

Slip the loop through the ring or around the bar from the front. Pull the ends through the loop and tighten ***(Fig. 11)***.

Fig. 11

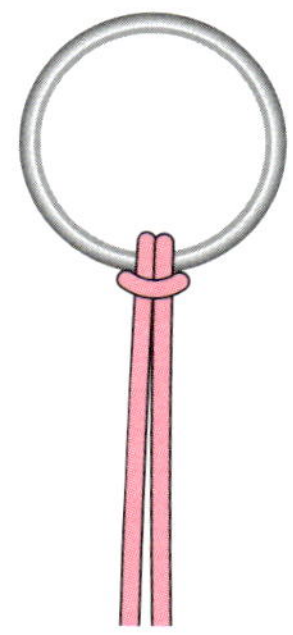

Making A Tassel

Wrap floss around the cardboard the specified number of times. Trim the floss from the skein. Slip a 16" length of floss behind the wraps and bring it to the top of the cardboard; tie a secure knot. Cut the floss loops on the end opposite the knot ***(Fig. 12)***. Remove the cardboard.

Fig. 12

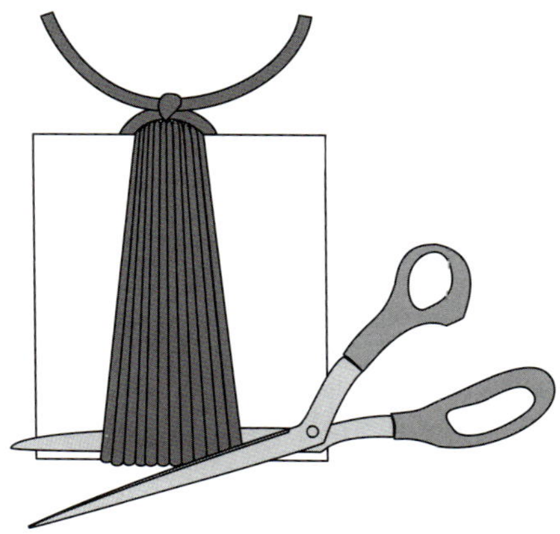

Form a loop with a 12" floss length. Wrap the floss around the loop and tassel neck about 1/2" below the knot ***(Fig. 13)***. Bring the end through the loop ***(Fig. 14)***. Pull firmly on the opposite end until the floss end disappears. Add a drop of adhesive to the back of the wrap.

Fig. 13

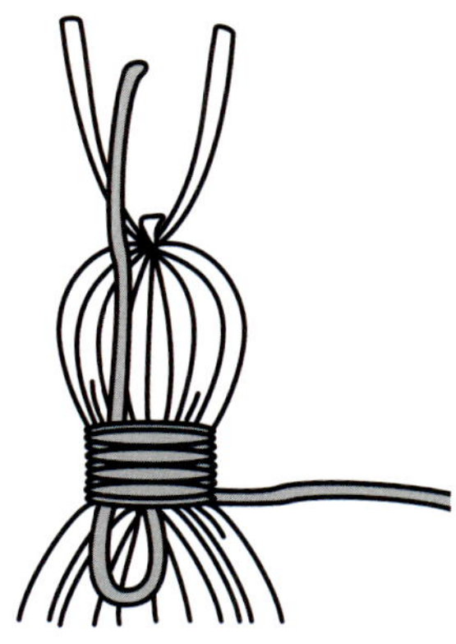

Fig. 14

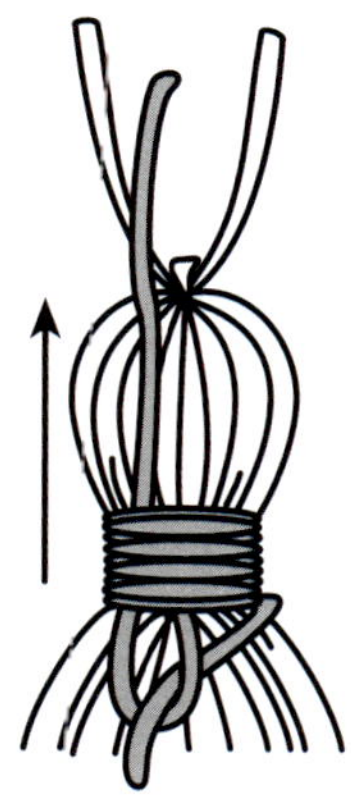

Meet Lori Wenger

"I've always been a designer of some form or fashion," says Lori Wenger. "And when the opportunity arose for me to design jewelry, I took it on as a new exciting challenge!"

Lori says her tasseled jewelry pieces were designed to be subtle statement pieces that can be dressed up for a night out or dressed down with jeans and a tee.

"I tried to design for a variety of styles but with one cohesive feel. But my personal favorite is the natural stone necklace because I am always inspired by natural tones and textures."

Lori was a Leisure Arts staff designer for more than seven years, contributing to books in The Spirit of Christmas and Gooseberry Patch series, among others. Since 2012, she has been a contributing photostylist for numerous Leisure Arts publications.

"My freelance career allows me to work in many different creative genres, from the photo styling, to illustrating, to designing. And luckily I have the continued support of a loving husband and two beautiful children."

More of Lori's creations may be found on Instagram: lori_wenger.

Production Team: Technical Writer – Mary Sullivan Hutcheson; Technical Associate(s) – Lisa Lancaster; Editorial Writer – Susan Frantz Wiles; Senior Graphic Artist – Lora Puls; Photostylist – Lori Wenger; Photographer – Jason Masters.